William Harcourt Sawyer

German field exercise 1888

Part II: The fight

William Harcourt Sawyer

German field exercise 1888
Part II: The fight

ISBN/EAN: 9783337149222

Printed in Europe, USA, Canada, Australia, Japan

Cover: Foto ©ninafisch / pixelio.de

More available books at **www.hansebooks.com**

LONDON: EDWARD STANFORD,

26 & 27, COCKSPUR STREET, CHARING CROSS, S.W.

1888.

CONTENTS.

PREFACE.

THE German Field Exercise, 1888, is divided into three parts.

The first deals with the details of drill, the second treats of the handling of troops in action and their previous training for war, and the third part embraces parade movements.

The first and third parts apply more particularly to the German army, whereas the second is of general interest to soldiers of all nations, being the most recent exposition of the most approved principles of modern European fighting.

The following three main conditions of success are brought prominently forward :—

1. The Commander-in-chief's intentions should be carried out in their integrity.

2. Subordinate Commanders, in co-operat-

ing to this end, should be given a free hand within their own sphere of action.

3. The thorough training for war of the individual soldier, with a view to qualifying him for assuming responsibility, and acting independently when necessary with judgment and decision.

W. H. SAWYER,

Capt. " The King's Own,"
Brigade Major, 1st *Brigade.*

October, 1888. *Aldershot.*

NOTE.—The words in large type are printed in a similar manner in the German original.

I issue to the Army this new Infantry Field Exercise, in grateful memory of His late Majesty, my Father, at whose instigation it has been produced. Its object is to provide a larger scope for war training, at the same time maintaining the discipline and order which have been handed down to us.

The advantage gained by the simplification of many of the formations, should on no account be nullified either by verbal or written additions to the Regulations by any one, for the purpose of obtaining increased outward uniformity, or for any other reason.

The freedom intentionally allowed, in the training and its application, should not be limited by any restrictions affecting the principles of the Regulations.

I am firmly resolved to punish with dismissal any contravention of this my will.

Any infringement of the provisions of Parts I. and III. will meet with severe censure, while any misapprehension of Part II. should be rectified by instruction.

(Signed) WILHELM.

To the
War Ministry.

INTRODUCTION.

1. THE object of drill is to train and prepare both officers and men for war. All exercises should therefore be in conformity with war practice. The most important requirements of war are strict discipline and order, together with the utmost exertion of mental and physical powers. The development of these qualities to such a degree that they become a second nature to the men, is one of the principal objects of all exercises at drill and field practices.

It is only by simplicity that results are ensured in war. It therefore becomes merely a question of mastering and practically applying a few simple formations. These, however, should be practised with strictness, and directed with certainty and precision. The provisions of the Regulations deal solely with normal formations, and are unconditionally binding in their spirit and letter, in peace or in war. All artificial elaboration is prohibited.

2. All Commanders of troops, from the Company Commander upwards, are responsible that the training of the units under their command is carried out in accordance with the Regulations, and should therefore be restricted as little as possible in the choice of means. Their immediate superiors are **in duty bound** to interfere, the moment they notice any errors or shortcomings.

3. The mastering of the actual drill should be **accomplished in the Company.** Battalion drill embraces only close formations, Regimental and Brigade Drill merely formations of assembly.

The **Battalion** is the **training school for the fight.** The whole system of Infantry fighting, is based on the co-operation of the several Companies with one another in the various phases of the fight.

The uniform education necessary for undertaking the duties connected with the training and leading of troops, is imparted, in the **Regiment.** Regimental, and more particularly

Brigade exercises are a preparation for the duties of higher commands.

Commanders of all grades are, however, responsible that every part of the Field Exercise is practised, and that the spirit of its provisions is fully carried out.

4. Continuous practice of one and the same exercise, wearies both body and mind. The exercises should therefore be varied. Their duration and description should also be suited to the powers of the men, otherwise their energies become inevitably relaxed, which produces an unfavourable effect on discipline.

5. The training on the drill ground should be supplemented, as often as possible, by a variety of operations on different descriptions of ground. Wherever the state of the crops renders this difficult during the finer seasons of the year, the late autumn and winter should be devoted all the more to the execution of these practices.

6. Exercises with troops at war strength, are also of the greatest value. They should be carried out at all times of the year, both at drill and field practices.

7. The **words of command** are composed

of two parts, cautionary and executive. The former part is delivered slowly, the latter sharply. The requisite pauses are indicated in the Field Exercise thus —. Slack words of command result in slackness of execution. Words of command should therefore be given in a similar manner and with equal smartness in all cases—in every place and on all duties.

Officers may indicate the direction of march, or order a halt, by means of signals with the sword. In the latter case the sword should be raised and immediately lowered. For the purpose of indicating the rallying point to an extended line, the sword should be kept raised. Further signals, for the purpose of carrying out particular measures, require to be specially pre-arranged by Commanders. In the fighting-line, the **whistle** is used to order the cease fire, and to attract the attention of the men to any order about to be given.

8. A uniform method of giving orders is enjoined throughout the army, in order that, in case of a change of Commanders, the dispositions made should be understood by the troops. **Such words of command (and signals) only, are therefore sanctioned, as are**

laid down in the Field Exercise. Should those words of command prove insufficient to meet any particular case, the issue of **orders** should be resorted to (see Field Service Regs., 1887, Part I., para. 4).*

* It should be regarded as an invariable rule, that an order should comprise everything, but no more, than that which a subordinate is unable to arrange for independently, with a view to attaining the prescribed object. The order should therefore be short, clear, and distinct, as well as adapted to the recipient's range of vision.

PART II.

THE FIGHT.

A.—GENERAL PRINCIPLES.

INTRODUCTION.

1. The thorough mastery of the simple formations laid down in Part I., forms the basis for a careful and uniform training of Infantry. This training would, however, fail in its main object, were it not to go hand in hand with an intelligent application of these formations to the **requirements of war.**

2. It is of course impossible to reproduce the conditions of the battle-field to their full extent on the drill ground. Besides the casualties, the usual sensations are wanting, which in reality exert such a detrimental influence. These will, as a rule, cause a lowering of the ideal performance of the troops, and the measure in which this occurs, depends

B

upon the morale of the troops and the amount of the loss sustained.

3. To establish and to raise the morale of the troops is, therefore, one of the principal objects to be attained by the training in time of peace, and all available means should be employed to this end and to the maintenance of discipline. This will be achieved in a great measure, by strict adherence to the several formations at **all** practices.

4. The requirements of war are **in no way** represented, but rather misrepresented by any neglect of these considerations on the drill ground.

The normal formations should be given up without hesitation, whenever the varying circumstances of the fight require it. But discipline and order should never be lost, even when different units become mixed up.

5. The requirements of war are fulfilled, according to this, when the **proper formations are adopted** for attaining the objects invariably resulting from the situation assumed. The formation selected, should be such as would be ordered in war to insure the highest fire action and which would be permitted for the purpose of reducing the effect of the enemy's fire. Whenever these two conditions are fulfilled (the former of which is always the more important), the practice is in conformity with the requirements of war. The more logical the progress, in this spirit, from the elementary to the more advanced exercise, the more surely will the prejudicial impressions experienced during the fight be overcome.

THE USE OF THE DRILL GROUND.

6. First and foremost the regulation formations should be practised on the drill ground.

7. Every **fight** should be conducted in accordance with the **object** in view, the available strength and time, and the nature of the ground.

The first of these factors is the ruling one, and exercises the most influence in forming plans. It determines the adoption of the offensive or the defensive, or a withdrawal, conducted under given conditions and lines of direction.

The object in view, is principally illustrated on the drill ground, and to this is due the special value of the exercises conducted thereon.

The application of the authorised formations on the drill ground is, however, limited to those practices which are intended to illustrate general tactical principles in the deployment and subdivision of troops and in the conduct of the fight. For this purpose, the nature of the ground should not be considered, and it is possible to do so, because the selection of suitable formations, depends more on the special character of the tactical task imposed, and on the relations to the other units, than on the peculiarity of the ground.

8. This rule, however, does not preclude advantage being occasionally taken of the formation of the ground as in war. Where the possibility exists of practising on the drill ground under assumed conditions, the attack of a height, a village, or a wood, the disposition for the defence of a ridge, the advance or retreat through a defile, it would be a neglect of favourable circumstances, if the most were not made of the opportunity offered.

As it is, however, more important to accomplish the object of the fight, than merely to take advantage of the ground, practices having the former object in view should be more frequent on the drill ground than the latter.

The fact should be intimated to the troops being exercised, whenever it is intended to take the formation of the ground into consideration.

9. By making this use of the ground there is, of course, a lack of **variety.**

The natural objects always remain the same for the same garrison. Special care should therefore be taken to prevent a certain set of tactical ideas becoming habitual, with the result that the practices carried out develop into local tactics, which would eventually degenerate into lifeless forms.

On the other hand, the desired variety may be obtained by means of **simple** suppositions capable of being generally understood, as to the existence of any particular description of ground, a defile, &c.

10. In any case, the frequent execution of field-practices is necessary, in conjunction with the exercises conducted on the drill ground. The troops will derive most profit from the practices off the drill ground, when the foundation has been laid by means of previous exercises on the drill ground, for the thorough grasp of the ruling principles and of the relative value of the formations to be adopted. A change from the drill ground to the country commends itself also for inspections, where such a procedure obtains.

11. For tactical exercises of every description, it is advisable to indicate the enemy's

position, if even by means of a few men and
some flags. *Occasionally, the strength of the
enemy may be increased with a view to repre-
senting the positions and movements of the
troops in rear of his position.   It is likewise
admissible, occasionally to exercise two
approximately equal forces in operating
against each other.

EXTENDED AND CLOSE ORDER.

12. Infantry should be able to fight over
any description of ground practicable for an
active man, and to surmount obstacles even
of a serious nature, when fully equipped.
Extended order is specially adapted for this
purpose.

**13. The Infantry fight will as a rule be
decided by fire action,** and this is most fully
developed in extended order.   The delivery of
fire by bodies in close order, is the exception.

14. Large bodies in close formation, are
liable to suffer very heavy losses in a short
space of time when within the enemy's effective
infantry fire.   This renders it necessary that
the brief moments favourable for their actual
insertion into the fight, should be seized with
accuracy.   The action of the fighting line, on
the other hand, may be extended over hours.

15. The uniform action, exercised by the commander of a large mass compressed, whether in depth or breadth, into a restricted space, is the object of **close formations.** Formerly, the only limit restricting the size of a body of troops, was the distance the word of command could travel. The increased effect of fire, now necessitates a further subdivision of bodies in close formation.

16. In **extended order,** the soldier is not rigidly bound to a fixed place or position of the body, or to the prescribed motions in handling the rifle. On the other hand, sound judgment, physical activity, boldness and self-reliance, great dexterity in the use of the rifle and in taking advantage of the ground, together with unremitting attention, are now required of him by his leaders.

17. Intersected and close country, as well as the noise and other dissolving influences of the fight, increase the difficulty of leading troops in extended order. This difficulty greatly increases the labour of training. It is during the fight in extended order, therefore, that it becomes most apparent whether troops have been thoroughly trained and disciplined, for a decrease of the commander's direct influence on the leading of the troops, is

accompanied by increased demands upon the
independent action of the individual soldier.

18. Fighting in extended order and the
correct application of its various formations,
passing from extended to close order and *vice
versâ*, require, therefore, to be practised more
thoroughly than the application of close
formations, in which the Infantry fight was
formerly conducted, extended order then
taking merely a secondary part.

19. Extended order, is the formation now
principally employed in action.

The fight is commenced, and in most cases
carried through to the end, in extended order.

**The extended line becomes, therefore, the
principal fighting formation of Infantry.**

20. **Close formation** nevertheless still retains its full use in the case of troops held in
readiness for action, and for reserves and
supports to the fighting line. It also gives
an impulse to the fight which in certain cases
determines the final issue. In the first line,
close formation will, however, only be used in
exceptional cases. But an action can never be
fought out to the end in close formation alone,
without the employment of extended order.

FIGHTING IN EXTENDED ORDER.

General Observations.

21. The increased importance of the fighting-line, imparts a special significance to its leading. The freedom of movement and the independent use of his rifle, which the soldier is allowed in the fighting-line, tend to render him more qualified and capable for the performance of his duties.

During his training, the soldier should be made aware of the fact that his duties when fighting in extended order, differ from those in close formation. It should be clearly impressed upon him, that **he can only do really good service under all circumstances, by exerting his powers to the utmost.** Being allowed greater freedom of movement, he should always be on the alert, and ever ready to take rapid and well-considered independent action.

It is the officer's duty to develop the judgment and self-reliance of the soldier, by means of instruction suited to his powers of understanding, and above all to convince him, **that the soldier's greatest danger lies in turning his back to the enemy.**

Extension.

22. Every engagement, is commenced by throwing out troops in extended order.

The primary object is to gain touch with the enemy, retaining at the same time perfect freedom of action. Only a small number of men should, therefore, be extended at first, and that **without hurry.**

A further reason for covering the advance by a weak extended line, such as is usually required at the outset of a fight, is to avoid surprise. In case the troops are surprised, notwithstanding this precaution, the first thing to be done is to regain freedom of action, by **rapidly** opposing the enemy with an equal force.

23. The forming of further plans, will depend upon whether it is intended to fight a containing or a decisive action. In the latter case, as soon as a clear estimate has been formed, of the numbers required for the successful issue of the operation, there should be no hesitation in deploying the necessary force and inserting it into the fight, in a formation favouring effectual co-operation. No greater fault can be committed, than to commence an action with **insufficient** forces, with the intention of reinforcing them by degrees. It amounts to continually engaging superior with inferior forces, and voluntarily relinquishing the advantages due to superiority of numbers. The failure of an operation entails not only **useless** losses, but also a deterioration of the morale of the troops.

24. Every engagement intended to be of a decisive character, will entail the occupation of the entire space available for deployment by a dense fighting line.

The extent of this space, depends upon the nature of the ground and the neighbouring troops engaged.

25. A comparatively narrow front is required at the commencement of the fight, for the prosecution of which, the commander intends retaining the greater portion of his force. The fighting line may be of various density at first. In any case, on entering upon a fight likely to prove long and costly, the front should not be increased to such an extent as to preclude its being occupied with a fighting-line of constant density and maintaining its full fire-action throughout. According to this, a company at war strength in extended order should not occupy a front **much exceeding 100 metres.***

* 109·3 yards.

Even during tactical manœuvres, a normal front of 100 metres should be allowed for a company in extended order. This extension, as compared with the strength of the company, is greater than that adopted in war. This, however, is equalised by the fact that the fighting-line is not thinned by casualties as in war.

26. A rigid adherence to the regulated **intervals in the fighting-line,** should never be insisted on.

The men are, on the contrary, to be distinctly instructed to close up or open out for the purpose of availing themselves of cover, especially when the extension is followed by an advance, during which they are unable to continue firing. Neither the direction nor the rate of advance should, however, be allowed to suffer thereby, and the total length of the line should not be appreciably increased.

27. Careful attention to **dressing,** is of even less consequence than the preservation of intervals. The only thing to be considered in this respect, is that the several portions of the fighting-line do not interfere ₁with one another in their movements and fire.

In the case of smaller units, still beyond the sphere of the enemy's influence, this in no way precludes a part of the fighting-line being ordered to direct, with a view to facilitating their advance.

28. When the fighting-line is approaching the position to be occupied, or when the extension takes place on the position itself, the subordinate Commanders should lead their parties in such a manner as to enable each soldier to take up such a position within the space available, as will afford him the best field of fire and cover.

Should the flanks remain unprotected either by other troops or by natural obstacles, a few men under an intelligent leader should invariably be despatched, as a **fighting patrol,** to keep up a sharp look out on the flanks.

29. Reinforcements become necessary, when the fire-action of a fighting-line, which has suffered, requires to be sustained or increased, or when a fresh impulse is needed to enable it to continue its advance.

Fire Action.

30. The action of Infantry consists primarily of the fire of the extended fighting-line. It is able, solely by its fire, not only to repel the enemy and prepare the attack, but also under certain circumstances, to decide the issue. In most cases, an overwhelming fire, concentrated on the decisive tactical points up to within short range, will produce such an effect that when the final rush is made, the position will be found to be either evacuated or only weakly held by the enemy.

Such fire-action requires coolness and dexterity in shooting on the part of the soldier and **fire discipline.**

31. The fire-effect of entire fighting-**lines,** depends upon the direction of the combined performances of a large number of rifles.

The simultaneous employment of the same kind of fire, by the several portions of the line, is not required. The indication, as an exceptional measure, of particular objectives to different units, requiring the employment of special descriptions of fire, is not precluded.

32. The proper moments for using the magazine are :—

In the attack : in the final preparation for the assault.

In the defence : in repelling the enemy's advance to the assault.

In receiving a charge of cavalry and on all other occasions during the fight, when a sudden and direct collision with the enemy occurs (attack and defence of works, localities, woods, &c.)

In firing on a retreating enemy.

Magazine-fire is only used in combination with the fixed sights, and the small flap.* It is only exceptionally employed at ranges between 800 and 300 metres,† when brief opportunities occur of firing at particularly important objects and increased fire-action is ordered.

The employment of magazine-fire, under circumstances justifying its use, is frequently left to the discretion of the individual soldier. In order that the highest capability of the rifle may not be prematurely exhausted, the individual soldier should be thoroughly trained to retain the magazine for those moments, in which it is desired to press the fight to an immediate issue, or when it becomes necessary to ward off some threatening danger.

33. It should be regarded as an invariable rule, with regard to the employment of fire, that it is only of a decisive nature, when **delivered at such ranges as will insure its**

---

* "German Muskt. Regs.," para 28.
　　Fixed sights used up to 200 m. (219 yards).
　　Small flap　　　" 　　　300 m. (328 yards).
With the new M-71 powder, at average temperature, by making a slight allowance, up to 250 and 350 m. resp.
　† 875–330 yards.

taking effect on the enemy's troops. To which arm these belong, is not a matter of primary consideration. In the majority of instances, the enemy's infantry would be the most important and profitable objective: at the same time, firing at batteries should not be overlooked. The choice of objects to fire at, is primarily decided by their temporary tactical importance. The next objects to be selected are those which, owing to their height, depth, width, and density, offer a prospect of high results.

Good troops should be capable, when their own fire does not promise to be effective, of **remaining under the enemy's fire without replying to it.**

34. It is only in very rare cases, that the employment of **indirect fire** should be attempted, and even then, only when known ranges and the stationary character of the object with regard to the curvature of the the trajectory, render a proportionate result probable, for example against troops behind entrenchments.

35. As a rule, the direction of the firing is confined to those commanders who are in the fighting line itself, namely the Zug * and Com-

* Pronounced " tsoog."

pany leaders. Other duties devolve on the higher Commanders in action, which they are not permitted to neglect by intruding into the sphere of their subordinates' command. They can only co-operate, by despatching the requisite forces to those parts of the fighting line, whence they intend to produce increased or concentrated fire-action.

In peace-manœuvres, however, the higher Commanders should take care that the direction of the firing, is properly attended to by the subordinate leaders.

36. The direction of the firing during the course of a fight, can frequently be but imperfectly carried out, owing to the casualties among the leaders in the fighting-line, which vary according to circumstances. But even then, the **fire-discipline** of the men who are left more or less to themselves should be maintained. Among properly trained and disciplined troops, the judgment of the individual soldier and the example given by the men of superior intelligence and courage, exert a powerful influence on the conduct of the fighting-line, and thus render the successful continuance of the fight possible, against an enemy who will by this time, find himself in an equally difficult position.

37. It should be borne in mind from the very beginning of the fight, that the **amount of ammunition carried is limited,** and its consumption represents an expenditure of power, which should only occur when most advantageous. On the other hand, should it be decided to direct the fire on any particular point, the full amount of ammunition required to fulfil the object of the fight should be used, as the tendency of an ineffectual fire, is to lower the morale of the troops and to raise that of their opponents. The judicious **husbanding of ammunition** is, therefore, an indispensable condition, especially at long and medium ranges, in order that the ammunition required to achieve success, may not be deficient at the critical moment.

The principles regulating the supply of ammunition in action, are laid down in the Field Service Regs., 1887, paras. 313 to 321.

Movements.

38. The movements of an extended fighting-line, are executed on the supposition that it is in contact with the enemy. They should therefore be **extremely simple.**

Beyond the range of the enemy's fire, the main points to be attended to, are the maintenance of order and connection. Within the sphere of the enemy's fire, the principal consideration, is to get at the enemy by the shortest way.

39. When advancing or retiring, the preservation of the proper **direction**, is of primary importance. Slight changes of direction, may be effected by **inclining** to the right or left, as long as the enemy's fire is not too severe. Extensive **flank movements** under fire, are not permissible.

Changes of front under fire, should be quite the exception. Should it become necessary to form a fighting-line to another front, a fresh line is formed in the required direction from the closed bodies in rear, that portion of the old fighting-line, which may no longer be required, being withdrawn.

40. The movements of the fighting-line are executed, as a rule, in quick time. When it becomes a question of reaching a certain point before the enemy, or of crossing spaces swept by the enemy's fire, it is done at the double. When the distance to be crossed is long, after proceeding a certain distance at the run, it may be necessary to make a halt, during which the men should lie down. When within effective range, a further advance is prepared by fire during the halt. In executing the **advance by rushes,** one portion of the fighting-line should keep up its fire, under cover of which the other portion will be able to advance. The distance covered in each rush, when in the presence of the enemy, depends upon a great variety of circumstances (nature of ground, composition of troops, severity of enemy's fire).

41. It should be borne in mind, that the advance is very apt to slacken when employing this method of attack, notwithstanding the large expenditure of strength entailed.

The great difficulty, which increases with every rush, of getting a fighting-line to advance from cover to cover when under a heavy fire, should cause the advance by rushes to be employed with caution. Should the enemy's fire admit of it, **the advance should be continued uninterruptedly.** At drill, therefore, the advance by rushes should neither be commenced too soon, nor practised as the only suitable formation for advancing over level ground.

Everybody should rather be thoroughly imbued with the idea, that the desired result can only be secured by **continuous pushing on to the front,** combined with well-considered preparation by fire ; and that, on the other hand, prolonged delay under the fire of a well-protected opponent, must necessarily entail heavy losses ; and, finally, that a retirement is synonymous with annihilation.

42. The most favourable circumstances for an uninterrupted advance, are those under which the enemy's fire can be kept down by superior fire, from a flanking or commanding position.

43. Firing on the move, produces an insignificant effect owing to the difficulty of handling the rifle steadily, taking a good aim, and making careful observations whilst in motion. It is, therefore, only applicable under special circumstances, for example, in order to prevent the undisturbed delivery of the enemy's fire, during a retirement of the fighting-line.

Closing.

44. The fighting-line is closed up, at the conclusion of the fight or after the requisite fire has been delivered on the retreating enemy. During a retreat, closing is only possible after the enemy's pursuit has ceased.

45. Troops are closed on principle, facing towards the enemy ; when closing on the move, they face in the direction followed.

46. It is of no consequence in action, that every individual soldier and every small unit should resume their original places, but it is of importance that closed bodies should be collected rapidly.

PROCEDURE WHEN OPPOSED TO THE VARIOUS ARMS.

47. In the case of **Infantry v. Infantry** the result depends, apart from moral factors, on the musketry training, fire-discipline, and the direction of the firing.

The Commander's task is to bring as many rifles as possible into action, or to gain the upper hand by concentrating the fire-effect of extended lines on decisive points.

The application of this principle is rendered easier, when cover can be obtained from the fire of the other portions of the enemy's line.

48. The individual Infantry soldier should realise the fact, that he is more than a match for a Cavalry soldier, even on open and level ground, if on encountering him, he is in immediate readiness to open fire. He need not even hesitate to engage several at a time, if he retains his calmness and presence of mind, and uses his rifle correctly as a

repeater, without taking his eye off his oppo
nents.

**Infantry should remain convinced, that
it has nothing to fear from Cavalry, even in
superior numbers, if it retains its coolness
and firmness.** Every formation is suitable
for repelling Cavalry, which admits of its being
opposed by the well-aimed fire of masses at
the halt.

The most effectual manner of receiving
Cavalry, is **to bring the greatest available
number of rifles to bear upon it.**

Only those formations therefore (i.e. changes
of front) which favour this, need be executed
against Cavalry. Infantry that does not dare
to receive Cavalry in extended order, when
its flanks are protected by the fire of troops
echeloned in rear, would not find safety even
in square.

49. Extended Infantry, when running, are
at the mercy of Cavalry, whereas when firing
steadily, they can face a Cavalry charge with
the fullest confidence. If the ground affords
them cover and protection, their power is
increased. Infantry engaged with the enemy's
Infantry, should in any case endeavour to
avoid assuming close formation, even when
threatened by Cavalry. Infantry is able to

advance even in the open, without regard to the enemy's Cavalry, as long as the latter is not supported by superior Artillery or Infantry, or is in such superior numbers that it can attack simultaneously from different directions with several lines.

50. The adoption of the square formation, can only be considered suitable when required by special circumstances, such as when the troops have expended their ammunition; when they have been severely shaken by previous heavy losses during the fight; or when compelled to retreat over open ground in the presence of threatening Cavalry, superior in numbers.

Infantry engaged with Cavalry, should bear in mind that, in all other cases, the latter are justified in counting it as an advantage gained, as soon as they succeed in compelling them to discontinue their movements and to assume formations which will interfere with the development of the most effective fire-action.

51. **In engaging Artillery,** it should be remembered, that to this arm belongs the superiority of fire at long and medium ranges. It is only at about 1000 metres* that the

* 1094 yards.

relative conditions become equalised, and at the shorter ranges the Infantry gains the superiority.

Infantry should endeavour to get as close as possible to Artillery, by availing itself of the formation of the ground. Infantry fire should first be directed on any teams that may be visible, and then on the gunners. Cases may occur, in which Infantry may engage Artillery with effect at the longer ranges. This entails the expenditure of a considerable amount of ammunition. Infantry should never, however, consider it to be their duty, to take the place of, or to compete with, Artillery at long ranges. Such a procedure, only leads to waste of ammunition.

The Employment of Entrenching Tools.

52. The increased importance of **artificial cover,** is due to the fire-action of the modern rifle. Prepared at the right time and place, the service it renders the troops and their leaders is important, and at times indispensable.

It should, however, be subservient to the leader's plans, and should in no way govern them. The latter is the case, when the entrenchments are commenced before the

Commander's plans are definitely formed. The premature strengthening of ground is positively detrimental, and restricts freedom of movement.

Tactical training is required on the part of Commanders, in order to know **when** and **where**, as well as how, to entrench.

The simplest kind of artificial cover is the **shelter trench**, which at first is intended for men lying down, and, if time admits, is deepened and strengthened for firing kneeling and standing. They are constructed in accordance with the instructions laid down for the training of Infantry in Field Engineering.

On the defensive, the pacing and marking of distances, should be combined with the construction of entrenchments. Even in the attack, entrenching tools may be of great service in the retention and strengthening of positions gained.

The construction of shelter trenches, either on or off the drill ground, is frequently impracticable, even when required by the assumed tactical situation, owing to circumstances which have to be considered in time of peace. In such cases the construction of shelter trenches should, at least, be indicated by taking all the necessary preliminary steps.

The Duties of Officers and Men in Action.

The Officer.

53. The difficulty of commanding troops, increases in proportion as the possibility diminishes of exercising a personal control down to the lowest ranks, and of effectively delivering words of command. The method of issuing orders should therefore be such, as to facilitate the attainment of the desired object in action, and this depends to a certain extent, on the suitable **selection of the Commander's place.**

Orders should therefore be issued by Commanders during peace manœuvres, from **the same place** and in the same attitude, **as in war.** A Commander may always make himself and his subordinate commanders exceptions to this rule whenever, and to whatever extent, he may consider it an advantage in the training of the troops. By occasionally dismounting, however, mounted officers will learn fully to realise and overcome the difficulties of command, and the men will become accustomed to seeing their leaders dismounted under a heavy fire.

54. When fighting in extended order, the attention of officers of all ranks should be particularly directed to the maintenance of connection, order, and command. Besides this, the **higher Commanders** should take care that the troops do not escape from their control, and the **subordinate Commanders** should endeavour on the accomplishment of their task, to rejoin the body of troops they belong to, or to place themselves at their disposal.

These conditions, will be fulfilled when the higher Commanders **refrain from ordering more** than they **should** or **could** order, and when the executive Commanders unite in working for the attainment of the appointed object, and abstain from abusing the independence accorded to them.

The exercise of **independence** within these limits, is the **foundation of great results in war.**

These considerations are applicable to the lowest rank of Commanders.

55. The **Zug leader** should take up such a position as will enable him to superintend the fire-action of his men. He arranges the disposition of his Zug in the space allotted to it, and decides on which objects the fire is to be directed, either in accordance with his instructions or on his own responsibility. He follows closely, the measures taken by the enemy and endeavours, according to his ability, to co-operate with the adjoining Züge in the fighting-line. He endeavours to ascertain, previous to a further advance, how the fighting-line, or portions of it, could be brought up closer to the enemy ; whether, or in what manner, a turning movement could be initiated ; or whether advantage could be taken of any exposed point in the enemy's line. The Zug leader in the fighting-line, will best be able to observe any opportunity of seizing an advantageous position, or of gaining an advantage over the enemy. He should then make up his mind how far. he should, **on his own responsibility**, turn such advantage to account.

56. The **Group leader** assists the Zug leader, and is responsible in his own sphere, for the placing of the men, for the adjustment of the sights, the proper handling of the rifle, the consumption of ammunition, and the replenishing of the magazine.

The Soldier.

57. The soldier generally goes into action after harassing exertions and marches, which are rendered more trying by the privations of war. He should, even under such circumstances, retain his energy, ·courage, calm judgment, and his power of rapid decision. These qualities, of which he stands most in need in moments of imminent peril, should be developed by the training he receives.

The man whose firmness of character, independence and disregard of self, are thoroughly developed by sound training, who by gradual preparation is able to undergo severe bodily exertion, and who is well instructed in the simple rules applicable to the various incidents of the fight, will also be able successfully to overcome the powerful emotions produced by the Infantry fight, and to behave as a reliable soldier in action.

58. During the advance, he must bear in mind that he is not to halt without a direct order, however severe the losses or the fire may be. Running to the rear leads to annihilation. On the other hand, **an attack really pushed home with determination, will always succeed.**

59. On the **defensive**, he should not move from the spot he is ordered to hold. He should do this with all the more confidence, knowing that his fire becomes the more annihilating the nearer the enemy approaches. The soldier should therefore preserve his ammunition for firing at short ranges, and then use it with certain effect.

60. Every soldier should endeavour to remain with the body of troops to which he belongs. Whoever is found remaining in rear of the fighting-line to which he belongs, without orders or without being wounded, or whoever carries wounded out of action without orders, is guilty of cowardice. Any man who has become separated from his company during the fight, should immediately attach himself to the nearest body of troops in the fighting-line, place himself under the orders of the officer or non-commissioned-officer in command, and render him the obedience due to his own superior. After the fighting is over, every soldier who has lost his corps, should look for it, and rejoin it without delay.

61. Men who in the stress of the fight, feel that their determination and judgment are deserting them, should look to their officers. Should there no longer be any present, there will be plenty of non-commissioned-officers and brave men, whose example will assist them in recovering themselves.

EXTENT OF FRONT AND SUBDIVISION.

62. The extent of front taken up by a body of troops, depends upon whether it has to fight by itself or in close connection with other troops. In the latter case, either one or both its flanks will be supported.

It further depends upon whether the fight is to be of an offensive or defensive character, or whether a retirement is intended.

63. The necessity for conducting an **independent** fight under varying circumstances, through the successive phases of its development, precludes the possibility of a simultaneous employment of the entire force in **a single** line, from the commencement.

As a rule it will be necessary to procure more detailed information, during the **preliminary operations**, of all circumstances that may tend to influence the **conduct of the fight.**

64. The **subdivision of troops in depth,** in at least **two bodies,** the leading one of which being the weaker and serving to open the fight, arises from this necessity alone. If these bodies succeed in clearing up the situation sufficiently to allow of the steps required for carrying through the fight being decided upon, a portion of the force should be held back in **reserve,** for the purpose of meeting unforeseen circumstances and bringing about a decisive result.

It resolves itself, therefore, into a depth formation in **three separate bodies,** and a yet further subdivision might become necessary under certain circumstances, such as the necessity for **special** flank protection. These additional subdivisions, however, should, if possible, be avoided, as the proper employment of the reserves generally renders them unnecessary.

65. The relative strength of the several bodies in the deep formation, cannot be laid down to meet all cases. **As a rule the leading body, whose duty it is to open the fight, should be as weak as possible, that retained as a reserve as strong as possible.** The former should generally not exceed, the latter not fall short of a quarter of the whole. These proportions are only meant to serve as a general guide, and should not lead to a breaking-up of corps.

66. It will not be possible to retain the adopted subdivision throughout the fight. In the first place, the body of troops told off to sustain the fight should co-operate with the one detailed to commence it, either all at once

or by degrees, and finally the reserve will be
utilised as required to confirm success or to
cover retreat.

This closing-up will nearly always cause
an increase of front.

67. For this reason alone, the **front taken
up** at the commencement of the fight, should
be a comparatively narrow one ; otherwise, the
front will be unduly extended during the
course of the fight, or a premature mixing up
of different commands will occur.

The question therefore arises in making the
preliminary arrangements for a fight : How
deep a formation **should** be adopted, and how
narrow a front **may** be taken up ?

Troops fighting independently, should bear
in mind that the extension of front only
furthers the desired result, when the flanks
are protected from turning movements.

68. In the case of troops associated **with
other troops,** being called upon to take part in
the fight, the extent of front to be taken up
will generally be given. The possibility of their
being threatened on the flanks, or even of being
able to deliver a flank attack, will invariably be
left out of consideration, when neither flanks
are exposed. These circumstances, point to
a disposition in which a larger force is thrown

into the fighting-line, and in which a special or particularly strong reserve is not required.

Troops supported on **both flanks**, are therefore justified in developing the strongest fighting-line; those supported on **one flank** only will, in the majority of cases, take up their deep formation and develop their front on the exposed flank.

69. Our Infantry, with its excellent musketry training, is able to repel any **front attack** by its fire. The enemy will suffer immense losses in the attack, and once repulsed, his confidence will be so severely shaken that he will hardly attempt to renew the attack.

70. Infantry which remains unaffected by losses due to the enemy's long-range fire, and receives his assault with a steady fire, is so strong in front, that if it avails itself skilfully of the advantages offered by the ground or by shelter trenches, will not require any direct support.

71. This Infantry has only **one** vulnerable spot, namely, the flank, as far as it is unprotected either by the ground or by other troops.

The **security of its flanks** exercises, therefore, a decisive influence on the result.

The most effective manner of securing the flanks, is by adopting a suitably organised

deep formation. But in this case, the principal consideration is where to post the troops retained in rear (Reserves).

72. They are liable to suffer severely from the fire directed on the fighting-line, if posted **in rear of its centre** in close formation. In order to withdraw them from this effective fire, they would have to be kept back so far, that the distance to be traversed would prevent their timely employment.

73. The **best position for the troops held in reserve is, therefore, in rear of the flanks of the fighting-line,** unless special circumstances require it otherwise.

74. The tactical situation and the nature of the ground, decide **as to the flank** in rear of which the Reserves should be kept. The flank on which the final decisive action is likely to occur, should be principally considered.

It should be noted, that loss of time is entailed by moving up the Reserves to a flank, which must, besides, as a rule, be performed under fire.

75. The **distances** to be maintained by the troops held in reserve, are regulated principally by the **object of the fight.**

Previous to entering into the decisive phase,

troops in close formation should, as far as possible, be kept under cover.

If it be determined to bring on the final crisis, the distances should be reduced during the course of the fight. All the Commanders, down to the lowest, should then be animated by a single desire, namely, **to be in front,** and to perform their part in securing the victory.

The crisis is generally of short duration, and in the few brief moments available, the troops still remaining intact must be disposed of as required.

Should it **not be intended to bring matters to a final issue,** the distances between the bodies in deep formation should be increased.

76. The distances depend, further, on the **ground.**

Open ground requires greater distances, and under fire, broader formations. (Strong fighting-line with line formation in rear).

If during the attack, it be found impossible to keep the lines in rear, out of the enemy's fire, care should at least be taken that two lines are not struck **simultaneously** by **one** Shrapnel shot, or by a **shower of bullets.**

The requisite distance is therefore increased

to over 200 m.*, which should only be lessened when the final issue is imminent.

Cover, admits of a reduction of distances. The Commanders should not fail to take advantage of this, as the rapid reinforcement of the advanced lines becomes more frequently necessary in this case. This holds good especially in wood fighting, in which, movements of closed bodies are principally confined to the roads.

When fighting in the dark, the relative importance of the various features of the ground undergoes a complete change, and the possibility of directing aimed fire on decisive points is precluded. **Offensive** operations, conducted without changing the direction of the advance, and with a very distinct objective previously indicated, are confined to short, well-known stretches of ground, as far as possible bounded on either side. Company columns in their simplest formations, placed abreast or in rear of one another, covered at a short distance by an extended line, is the best formation preparatory to a hand-to-hand fight, or for engaging in a vigorous musketry fight, with heads of columns at close quarters. Any further splitting-up of troops would be calculated to cause confusion. On the **defen**

* 219 yards.

sive, the object is to hold the position occupied, without a further subdivision of the troops.

The firing should be brief and severe, and only delivered at the shortest ranges. Arrangements should be made by daylight, to sweep the roads leading from the enemy by fire. When therefore, a night attack may be expected, the advanced line of outposts should be strengthened. The co-operation of the troops on either flank, is confined to unexpected flank attacks.

77. It becomes frequently necessary to reduce the distances on the drill ground, in accordance with the limited space available. Should this be unnecessary, it will be advantageous in the training of the troops, if the proper distances are maintained.

78. Troops in close formation have, as a rule, to conform to the movements of the fighting-line.

Their approach to the fighting-line, invariably indicates the approaching termination of the fighting. They may be employed either to reinforce the fighting-line, or for delivering the attack. In which latter case, they would retain their close formation.

The manner of their employment, depends upon the object of the fight, the time available, and other considerations.

ATTACK AND DEFENCE.

79. In the offensive, a fundamental distinction should be drawn between the attack of a fully developed front, well prepared for defence, and an encounter between troops in motion.

80. The encounter between bodies of troops in motion, so frequent in war, develops itself from the depth of the column of march, against an opponent who is likewise deploying for action.

In such engagements, the leading troops should gain the requisite time and space, to enable the columns to deploy.

On these occasions, the subordinate leaders should only exercise such a measure of independent action, as is admissible without interfering with the connection between the progressive deployment of the whole force, and that of the leading troops. It is in this spirit, that the Company at the head of the Battalion acts. The same occurs at head of the Advance Guard, &c. On the one hand, the object is to forestall the enemy in his deployment for the fight, whilst on the other hand, the independent action of the leading troops should be restricted, so as not to interfere with the intentions of the Commander.

It thus becomes apparent how important it is, that the commencement of an encounter between troops in motion, should find the Commander at the head of the column. The simultaneous issue of orders for the conduct of the fight, and for the deployment into position from column of route, will thereby be rendered possible.

The attack should be delayed as little as possible, by the deployment for the fight. Preparatory extensions at the halt, only cause delay.

The preliminary phases of our engagements, will generally bear this character.

81. Should the enemy have nearly completed his deployment, or should he be already partially in position, the extension of the foremost troops should be carried out with increased caution. The front should be increased by the continued deployment, and the Commander's orders should be awaited. In order to issue these in time, the Commander should unquestionably be on the spot.

82. The attack of a position completely occupied, and perhaps **prepared for defence,** should, on the other hand, be **planned** by the Commander from the very commencement. The independent action of the individual,

should not be allowed to cause the deployment
to be made at haphazard. The enemy has in
this case, clearly surrendered the advantage
of the attack, the Commander consequently,
gains the advantage of being in a position to
choose the direction and manner of his attack.
In such cases the deployment for the fight,
is made in accordance with the intentions
of the Commander, previous to commencing
the action.

The difficulty of crossing ground commanded by the enemy's fire, may render it
necessary to advance under cover of darkness.
In such cases, the troops would generally be
advanced the day before, as far as possible
without getting within range of the
enemy's fire, and the first line pushed forward
in the dark to such a position, as would enable
it to open fire at break of day.

A planned attack will only then have any
chance of success, **when it is able to secure
a superiority of fire.**

The superiority of Artillery fire is the first
thing to be aimed at. It prepares the ground
over which the Infantry attack has to advance.

Should the ground offer suitable rallying
points in front of the enemy's position, these
should be seized first. The larger deploy-

ments for the fight are effected in rear of such points. It is a rule for advanced troops, to endeavour to get up as close to the position as the ground will allow, in order to open fire.

Strong fighting-lines will work up gradually to the position, and endeavour to overpower the enemy with their fire. These will best be supplied by the troops whose duty it is to sustain the fight. When the fighting-line has succeeded in arriving within a short distance of the enemy, the supports, brought up as close as possible, should be ready for immediate action.

Until a superiority of fire has been gained, or the enemy appears to be seriously shaken, the assault can only be delivered at a heavy cost. The final stroke should therefore be deferred, until the necessary fire-effect has been attained,

The fighting-line will be the best judge of the results attained. It is the first to recognise when and where the enemy's resistance is decreasing; it is able to avail itself most quickly of any advantage gained ; the final assault will therefore frequently emanate from the fighting-line. It then becomes the duty of the supports at once to follow the fighting-line with a view to supporting it and to protecting it from counter attack. Generally, however, the Commander of the fighting-line should bear in mind, that the order to assault should be given by him, and at the right time. When the fighting-line has arrived to within short range of the enemy, and, having been sufficiently reinforced, has paved the way for the assault by the highest attainable fire-action, the bodies of troops echeloned in rear should be brought up to the foremost line without a halt, and together with it should deliver the final blow. The drums of all closed bodies, commence beating from the moment that the advance to the assault can no longer be concealed from view. Whether the closed bodies find themselves alongside or in rear of each other, what their formation is, and whether the Commander should still retain a reserve, depends entirely upon circumstances. In this most decisive moment of the attack there is only one watchword for a fighting-line, and that is " **Forward** "—Forward ! straight for the goal ! The beating of drums, the continuous sounding of the " **Rapid advance** " by all the buglers, sets everybody, even the hindmost, in motion, and with cheers, the assaulting troops throw themselves upon the enemy.

Any further addition to the rules laid down above, for regulating the procedure of attack is prohibited.

83. Procedure after a successful attack.— It is not sufficient to have captured the enemy's position—its retention should also be secured. This is effected by the pursuit of the retreating enemy, and by placing the points captured in a state of defence. Should villages, farmsteads, woods, &c., form part of the enemy's position, the attack on them should be pushed uninterruptedly through to the further boundary. The further pursuit does not, as a rule, consist of pushing on, but of firing on the enemy, during which time, the troops which have carried out the assault, occupy the position captured and re-form. They will thus, in a short space of time, be prepared for renewed operations.

84. The enveloping movement. — The superiority of fire essential to success, can be most easily secured by an enveloping movement. This should be provided for beforehand in the original dispositions, either by advancing from different directions, or by causing the troops in rear of the fighting-line to join in the attack.

Attempts at executing enveloping move-

ments with portions of the Infantry in the
foremost fighting-line, already extended and
probably even already engaged, where they are
not specially favoured by the ground, are not
likely to succeed, and lead to a mischievous
splitting-up of forces.

85. The defence.—No other kind of fighting
is so dependent on the formation of the ground
as the defensive.   To carry it out, localities,
heights, ravines, woods, defiles, &c., are required.

**The object to be considered in every
defensive operation, is the effective use of
fire.**   This point is the prominent consideration, in selecting and in artificially strengthening a position.

As soon as the direction of the enemy's
attack is ascertained, the fighting-line is fixed
at such a strength, from the very first, as may
appear requisite to maintain a firm hold on the
position, taking the ground and the object of
the fight into consideration.   Shelter-trenches
and other cover are prepared, the ranges to
important points are taken, ammunition is
distributed from the ammunition carts to the
troops, who, when posted, place it in a handy
position ready for use.

The supports are brought up, and in certain

circumstances are drawn quite close up to the fighting-line. The distances should be reduced. Reserves are kept back only so far as to be sheltered from the enemy's fire, but near enough to be close at hand for the defence of their respective sections.

The number and extent of the sections will vary in accordance with the nature of the position. The worse the interior communications, and the less the possible supervision of the position, the more numerous and the narrower the sections. For the occupation of the position, distribution in depth is the ruling condition. Each **section** is organised as a **separate command,** arranging for its own reserve. The following are the principal points to be considered in deciding upon the position for the **main reserve,** i.e. of those forces which are not tied down to a particular section of the position. The defence whose only object is to repel the enemy (outpost and rear-guard actions) can confine itself to maintaining its position. On the other hand, **the defence whose object is to achieve a decisive result,** must be combined with the attack. The pure defensive will never result in the annihilation of the enemy. In accordance with this, troops should be economised in the distribution for local defence, and the main reserve should be assembled at a point from which, owing to the general situation and the nature of the ground, an offensive movement could most readily be executed at any given moment. This, as a rule, will prove to be on one of the flanks. This arrangement is the best provision against enveloping movements, which are the greatest danger to which strong positions are exposed.

The larger the defending force, the greater should be the interval between the main-reserve and the flank. Greater space will thereby be afforded for deployment and advance to the attack, which would threaten that of an enemy in flank, and increase the security from enveloping movements.

A caution is necessary against completely occupying positions before the direction of the enemy's attack is ascertained.

86. No regulations can be made to meet the case of a **retreat,** after a defeat. The choice of direction in their retreat, no longer belongs to troops engaged with the enemy, when once repulsed or withdrawn. When followed up by the enemy, troops must retire without change of formation, perpendicularly to their front, and require to be relieved, in order to enable them to prepare for making a fresh stand. The deduction from this is, that a retreat can only be regulated when the troops are still in deep formation. It should, however, be remembered that it would be wrong for troops who are called upon to fight a decisive action, **to keep back a reserve for the purpose of covering their retreat, instead of employing it during the fight.** The Commander should make up his mind in good time, as to ordering a retreat, and taking the necessary measures for carrying it out.

The selection of a position for the relieving troops, should depend upon the resisting power of the troops engaged, but should be sufficiently near to save the retreating line from disorganisation. Relieving positions, are more favourably situated when taken up just on the flank of, than immediately on the line of retreat. The Commander details the troops intended for relieving purposes from that portion of his force, which is still intact. The troops occupying the relieving position, offer the enemy such opposition, as will afford the retreating force time and space to re-form unmolested. This condition, determines the duration of the resistance offered. Should there be no chance

E

of a timely arrival of fresh troops giving a favourable turn to the situation, the relieving troops must be withdrawn.

In most cases it would be necessary to take up another relieving position.

A well-conducted retreating action, should eventually lead to the formation of the column of march, with a properly formed rear guard. In ordering a withdrawal, the Commander should distinctly indicate the point on which to fall back, and order where, and by what troops, the relieving position should be taken up. The Commander will only be in a position to fulfil these duties, if, after having taken these measures, he leaves the scene of action and gives the withdrawing troops their respective orders in person. The rest is the concern of the subordinate commanders. Every unnecessary show of front, for the purpose of supporting troops occupying a relieving position, proves as a rule, a disastrous mistake, as it then becomes a matter of great difficulty to disengage troops from the fight.

87. These regulations, do not lay down either instructions or views for every description of fight. They do not deal with containing actions, feigned actions, or demonstrations. The conduct of such engagements, which varies considerably according to the situation, is in each case the business of the Commander.

It will always be necessary for the Commanders to decide, in the different cases, whether a formation of greater depth is to be adopted, and what extent of front is required for deployment.

B.—THE SEVERAL UNITS IN ACTION.

(Units of Command.)

THE COMPANY IN ACTION.

88. The Company should be capable of executing all the movements laid down (extending, closing, rapidly changing from extended to close order, and *vice versâ*, &c.) on a brief order or signal from its Commander.

Fighting in extended order requires, further, that every Zug, and each of its component Groups, be capable of finding out for itself the right way of executing the task imposed, or resulting from the tactical situation. As soon

as the object of the fight, renders it no longer
necessary for the Zug to remain extended,
it will, without waiting for the order, close
and rejoin the Company column. The
Group closes when it can no longer act, and
resumes its place in close formation, in the
rallying Zug. The practical execution of
this principle should, by practice, become a
matter of habit. When ordered to extend, the
Zug leader takes command of his Zug.
During the course of the fight, the Commander
has frequently no time at the right moment,
and still more frequently no means, for the
transmission of the order to change front or
close. At the end of the fight the Zug, and in ·
it the group, should nevertheless be found in
its right place. **Where** that is, cannot be decided beforehand.

89. The Company finds itself only exceptionally, when detached, in the position of
having to undertake a fight by itself. As a
rule, it fights as part of a Battalion. Whereas
the Company Commander has to work entirely
on his own responsibility in the execution of his
task when acting independently, when his
Company forms part of a Battalion, he is bound,
in making his dispositions, to consider his
connection with the other companies. The

latter case, demands that the Commander should not lose sight of what is going on near him, and in rear of him, notwithstanding that his attention is principally taken up by what is occurring in his front.

The fight of the Battalion should be considered as a whole, the limits of which should not be overstepped by any of its component parts. But even within these limits, the independence of the Company, of which it should not in any way be deprived, is great as soon as it enters into the fight. Orders from the rear are quickly overtaken by events. A constant waiting for orders, would render it impossible for the Company to act rightly, and at the proper moment.

The independent forming of plans should, however, always be regulated by the consideration, that the connection with the Battalion as as a whole, and the proper place in the same throughout all the varying circumstances, should be maintained.

90. The employment of a weak fighting-line at the **commencement of the action** is advisable, because with a strong fighting-line, a change in the dispositions or a change of front is always difficult, and when executed under fire, always accompanied with loss. As a rule, entire Züge are inserted by degrees into the fighting-line. Whereas the simultaneous extension of several Züge as a fighting-line, would only be ordered under special circumstances, the extension of only half a Zug, or even of a smaller party, is not precluded when the object is to secure the Company against surprise.

91. The **progressive development** of the fight entails an increase of fire-action in the foremost line, and, at the same time, the filling up of casualties. For this purpose, the fighting-line of a Company, may either be prolonged or strengthened by the insertion of reinforcements. The former procedure favours the proper exercise of command and fire-discipline, and should therefore, where practicable, be adopted. Notwithstanding this, the latter will be of more frequent occurrence, for when working in combination with other troops, the requisite space for the prolongation of the fighting-line will generally not be available. The Company should therefore, be so trained, that the complete exercise of command is not lost by the intermixture of men belonging to different Züge and Groups.

92. The extension of an **entire** Company should, if possible, be avoided, or at least

postponed as long as practicable. A Company
entirely extended, is no longer under the control of the Commander in an attack, and, even
when occupying a position, can no longer be
commanded by him as a whole. It is then,
still further withdrawn from the command of
the Battalion Commander. The Company
Commander should therefore aim at retaining
a closed body under his control, in rear of the
fighting-line, as long as possible. It is only
with this body, that he will be able to fill up
the casualties, to support the attack or
defence, or to ward off any threatened flank
attack.

93. The **support** of a Company, a portion
of which has been extended, will, as a rule, be
formed by the remainder. The formation of
a smaller intermediate support, between the
fighting-line and the main-body of the Company, becomes necessary when the close
proximity of such a body to the fighting-
line is required. The necessity of flank protection, may likewise lead to the posting of
special bodies in rear of a flank. Such a
subdivision is always disadvantageous, and
should therefore be restricted to exceptional
cases.

The respective distances of the closed bodies,

are regulated by the circumstances of the fight, and by the formation of the ground. **They should be such as to ensure the right-timed support of the fighting-line.** The choice of formation, is dependent on the ground and the enemy's fire. When visible by the enemy, the line is preferable; the column, on the other hand, can obtain cover more readily.

94. If required, the entire strength of the Company should be applied in order to **sustain the fight.** Finally, whether the whole Company should be extended in the fighting-line, or whether closed bodies should be ·employed at the last, depends upon the circumstances under which the Company is fighting. In any case, **the intensity of fire should be raised to the highest attainable pitch, which should, if possible, be maintained until the beginning of the end.**

An **isolated Company in action**, having to provide for its own support and flank protection, should employ the troops used for this purpose in close formation, which will be found most suitable whether on the offensive or defensive.

When **forming part of a Battalion**, the various duties of the attack and defence will be divided amongst the several Companies.

After the desired fire-effect has been produced, the assault is delivered at a smart run on the points indicated in the enemy's position.

95. The Commander should retain the control of his company during the fight. He conveys his intentions to the Zug leaders in the form of concise and clear orders, and then takes up such a position as will enable him to direct his Company. He arranges for the supply and distribution of the ammunition brought up from the rear, with all the means at his disposal on the battle field.

The Battalion in Action.

96. The Battalion possesses, in its four Companies, an organisation that enables it to adapt itself most readily to whatever task may be allotted to it in action.

The method adopted by the Commander in working his Battalion in action, is to assign tasks to the several Companies. Direct interference with the Züge of individual Companies, is only permitted when evident misunderstandings or mistakes, threaten to divert the course of the fight into improper directions.

It is the duty of the Battalion Commander at the commencement of the fight, to impart his orders briefly, clearly, and with precision to each one of his Company leaders—if possible in the presence of all—leaving the manner of execution to them.

He should be guided by this principle, throughout the course of the action. His endeavour should be, to maintain the co-operation of the several Companies with one another during the fight. The Companies on their part should strive equally to preserve this co-operation by accomplishing the tasks assigned to them.

The Battalion Commander has often no time, and still oftener no means, for the transmission of an order in proper time. The termination of the fight, should nevertheless find the several Companies at their right places. Where that is, cannot be decided beforehand.

97. The Commander will, in the majority of cases, do well to postpone the extension of **entire** Companies as long as possible.

Entirely extended Companies, are no longer under the control of the Commander, and even when occupying a position, can no longer be commanded by him as a whole. Should a strong fighting-line be required, it is preferable at once to make use of several Companies. forming their own support. This at the same time prevents, as far as possible, the premature mixing up of different Companies.

98. The disposition of the Battalion is regulated by the object of the fight and by the ground. No general rule exists, as to whether a Battalion should have its four Companies or only one in the front line. Whether it should enter into the fight formed in one, two, or three successive lines, the Commander possesses a free choice according to circumstances.

The entire Battalion may deploy for the fight at the halt, on any given Company, or, if required, it can take up its position on the move. The former will be the rarer case ; it should, however, be equally practised. None of the various formations should be turned into fixed rules.

99. In the majority of cases, it will be advisable to extend the Companies only as required, retaining the remainder of the Battalion in hand. For example, when a fight is commenced on the march, by the leading Company of the Advanced Guard, and it becomes necessary to extend their front to a flank, a second Company is employed for this purpose. If it can be gathered from the progress of the fight, on which flank the main body should be posted, or which flank is threatened, the troops remaining in hand will be formed up in rear of it. The circumstances which influence the manner of co-operation of the four Companies, as well as their extension and relation to each other during the fight, may vary considerably. The Battalion Commander will always be in a position to meet these circumstances, if he maintains a deep formation, and only employs his Companies where they are clearly required. He should employ a **sufficient** number of troops at the **proper time,** but should guard against their premature absorption.

100. The movements of a Battalion once extended, should be regulated by the indication of a point to march on. With regard to the amount of space occupied by a Battalion extended in action, it should be remembered that the greatest measure of extension is given by that of four Companies in a line. **In extending thus, however, the Battalion Commander manifestly surrenders an important share of his influence on the course of events.** But in the case of a Battalion fighting alone, when the required space is undoubtedly available, a narrowing of front and an increase in depth, is generally enjoined as the fighting formation. As a rule, therefore, the front occupied in action will be a narrower one.

The necessity for a deep formation, is greatest in defensive positions, for a Battalion fighting alone, and for extension at the commencement of the fight. The narrower the front taken up, the further should be the flanking troops from the flanks.

101. The only troops remaining at the disposal of the Battalion Commander for **carrying on the fight**, are those stationed either in echelon or in rear of the centre. It is with regard to these, that he selects his own position, which is only quite exceptionally in the foremost line, nearly always with the troops retained in rear, but in any case in some place whence he can exercise supervision over his Battalion in action.

He will frequently, only be able to affect the fire-action of the Companies, by directing the fresh supplies of ammunition to those points in the fighting-line, where it may be most needed.

102. Should a Battalion be drawn from the reserve, for the purpose of bringing the fight,

which has been prepared by the fire-action of other troops, to an immediate conclusion, it should endeavour to profit by its previous concentration.

In such cases the companies, opened out to short intervals from each other, are enabled to adopt a suitable fighting formation.

THE REGIMENT IN ACTION.

103. The Regiment, owing to its history, its training as a whole, the homogeneity of its corps of officers, and the number of its component parts (3 or 4 Battalions, as the case may be), is specially adapted for the independent execution of tasks that may be allotted to it in action. It is in the Regiment that the instinct of co-operation is keenest, and the Commander is assisted by its organisation in forming an accurate estimate of the reinforcements required in action. The Commander appoints to the Battalions their respective tasks, leaving them perfect freedom as to the manner of execution.

Interference with the conduct of individual Companies should be restricted to rare exceptional cases, and is only justifiable when the action of subordinate leaders threatens seriously to interfere with the execution of the Com-

mander's general intentions, and there is no
. time to issue the necessary orders through
the proper channel.

The Commander retains his controlling
influence on the Battalions employed in the
foremost line during the fight most effectually,
by allotting to them separate sections of the
positions when on the defensive, and when on
the march or on the offensive by giving them
respectively points to march on. This may
be done, according to circumstances, by indicating to Battalions a general point of direction,
situated at a sufficient distance from the front,
or by giving them separate objectives, or,
finally, by ordering one Battalion to follow
the required direction of march or attack,
directing the remainder to conform.

The co-operation of Battalions fighting
alongside each other, should be regulated by
directing their advance on some object in
their **front**, and never by causing them to
dress by a flank. Battalions, therefore, fighting alongside each other, will never be **dressed**
by a flank. On the other hand, it will doubt-
less be very frequently necessary, to order
connection to be kept up during the fight by
the centre or by a flank.

104. The forces kept in hand by the Regimental Commander, are the only means he possesses for developing the fight in depth or · breadth as required by circumstances, or in accordance with his intentions. He will never allow more Battalions to pass out of his control than are actually necessary for the progressive development of the fight. He thus retains control over that portion of the battle-field which falls to his share, and remains well prepared for the various contingencies of the fight. It is more particularly only in this manner that the enemy's flank can be turned, or his flank attacks warded off successfully. The Commander is only able to execute a fresh change of front by employing the Battalions retained in rear, those already engaged being tied down to their fighting front. The difficulty of pushing on the foremost fighting line, increases with the numbers employed.

The preliminary deployment for the fight, which should be prepared for by the Regimental Commander while still in column of march or formation of assembly, must therefore precede the accurate determination of the front to be occupied when in action. The disposition of the Regiment in breadth or depth, is regulated by the extent of this front and by the relative position of the Regiment to the neighbouring troops. The narrower the first deployment, the greater should be the interval between the bodies retained in rear.

105. It makes a considerable difference whether the Regiment enters into the fight from column of march, or from formation of assembly. The leading Battalion may, in the former case find itself already engaged by the time the next one arrives on the ground. A deep formation for the leading Battalion, and the earliest adoption of column formation for the remainder, with a view to shortening the column of route, is then rendered necessary. The deployment for the fight should already have been begun, during the advance to occupy the position indicated by Regimental Commanders.

106. A flank march in the presence of the enemy which might possibly become necessary, can only be conducted with sufficient safety, when the formation adopted at the commencement of the movement is such as to ensure a right timed and properly organised deployment towards the enemy. Such a flank march within effective range of the enemy could, however, only be carried out when covered by the formation of the ground.

F

107. A normal extension of front cannot be laid down for an Infantry Regiment. The extent of front it occupies, depends upon the nature of the unit of which it forms part, as well as upon the object of the fight, and the character of the ground. The extent of front of a Regiment fighting **alone,** on the other hand, should at the commencement rarely exceed that of two Battalions extended alongside each other.

108. In carrying out the attack, the Regiment once deployed, moves, as a rule, direct to the front. Should any inclination to a flank become necessary, it is indicative of a mistake committed in the original deployment. The remedy for such a mistake, lies generally in bringing up the troops echeloned in rear, but it will nearly invariably result in the weakening of the blow delivered.

109. For the due execution of the tasks imposed upon him, the Regimental Commander should take up a properly selected position. At the commencement, this will be in front, His presence is principally required there, in the case of an encounter between troops in motion. During the fight, he can generally direct his troops to the best advantage from the vicinity of the bodies echeloned in rear, that is, whence he can exercise the best supervision over the deployment of his Regiment· Should his Regiment be fighting in Brigade, he should select such a position as will enable him to keep up communication with the Brigade Commander.

THE BRIGADE IN ACTION.

110. The Brigade is the largest unit of command which it is possible to exercise on limited areas.

As a Battalion at war strength with its light baggage occupies 400 m.* of road, the distance taken up by a Brigade is so considerable, that the **character of the fight** is at times seriously affected thereby.

The action of the Brigade depends upon the time required for deployment, it is therefore **important** to keep in view the difference between the distances required by the same units at war strength, and on a peace footing.

111. It is only a Brigade composed of three Regiments, or of two Regiments and a Jäger Battalion, that possesses the advantage of a tripartition. When the subdivision is in two parts, the Brigade Commander will frequently

* 427 yards.

be compelled to set aside a reserve, according to the object of the fight—not less than one Battalion.

112. The best fighting-formation for the Brigade, is with its Regiments placed alongside each other, dividing the front occupied, and regulating their own reinforcements as required.

But the adoption of this normal formation is not always possible from the commencement, nor should the more important considerations bearing on the fight be sacrificed in the endeavour to assume it.

Occasionally, in the encounter of troops in motion, the needs of the foremost line may render the hurried adoption of a broad formation imperative, the majority of the Battalions of the leading Regiment being thus at once brought up alongside each other in the first line. Such circumstances render it specially necessary for these Battalions to arrange for their own supports and reserves, as the leading Battalion should never count upon the Battalion following it, being available for the support of its fighting-line. **The rule should be strictly adhered to under all circumstances, that each Regiment is to be allotted its own separate task, and that the Brigade Commander should confine himself to delivering**

his orders only to Regiments. The mixing-up of Regiments is disadvantageous, and should not, if possible, be resorted to.

In the majority of such cases, therefore, the Regiment next in succession in the column of route will form up in rear of one of the flanks, and will be kept there as a decisive reinforcement. The more circumstances may have necessitated a hurried deployment into a broad formation at the commencement, the more carefully should this reinforcement be there retained.

113. The Brigade is such an important body, owing to its fighting power and the space it occupies when deployed for fighting, or on the line of march, that it may fairly be required to fight simultaneously and as a body, in several directions. In this case the distances covered by its component parts, from their respective positions in the column of march previous to deploying in the required direction, are considerable. The moving to a flank of troops already deployed, is no longer possible in this instance. The Commander should bear in mind that the length of the Brigade column of route should be reduced in proper time previous to a deployment, by the deployment of its several parts and subsequent closing up

of the troops in rear. The several portions
will avail themselves of any halts that may
occur, for the purpose of obviating unnecessary delays in the deployment of the whole.

Together with the orders for the fight, the
Regiments are given their respective points of
attack, or sections of ground to be defended.
The better connected these are, the more complete will be the co-operation of the Regiments.

114. The selection of the Brigade Commander's position is of great importance and
should be changed as rarely as possible.

The commencement of an action should
find him at the head of his Brigade; for neither
reports, nor information, nor maps can take
the place of a personal inspection of the
enemy's position, that of the neighbouring
troops, or of the ground. In that position he
is best able effectually to direct the initial
deployment, on which the subsequent course
of the action so greatly depends. It likewise
enables him to seize advantages over the
enemy by arriving at timely decisions, to
ensure his troops taking the shortest routes,
to direct their action into proper channels, and,
finally, to prevent any irregular action on the
part of the commander of the advanced troops.

During the action, however, the Commander remains sufficiently in rear to enable him to exercise supervision over the several parts of his Brigade. This will generally be in the vicinity of the troops he has retained at his own disposal. It is only from there that he can still control the course of the fight. He delivers his orders, as a rule, to his immediate subordinates. Should circumstances compel him to deviate from this rule, and to give individual Battalions direct orders for the execution of urgent measures, he should at once inform the Regimental Commander of the fact, with whom he should maintain uninterrupted communication.

115. The average extent of front of a Brigade in action, may be deduced from experience gained in war.

A Brigade of six Battalions, in its initial deployment for the fight, has occupied a front of 1000—1200 metres.*

116. The execution of tactical exercises presents the greatest difficulty in the case of a Brigade, owing to the space required for its movements and deployments for action. The object to be attained on the drill ground, will not be so much the conduct of one fight in its

* 1094–1313 yards.

various stages, as the representation of a variety
of deployments under different suppositions.
Practice in adopting formations suited to the
object in view, forms the most important
tactical task of the Brigade. The conduct of
the fight, on the other hand, should, whenever
possible, be practised in the country.

C.—CONCLUDING REMARKS.

117. The simplicity of the formations and
rules laid down in these Regulations, must
favour thoroughness of training.

They suffice for the requisite uniform
training of the whole of the Infantry, and
their simplicity is a guarantee that the reserve men rejoining the colours on the order
for mobilisation, relearn them in the shortest
possible time. A close watch should, however,
be kept, **that the strict discipline developed
on the drill ground, is maintained so far as
circumstances admit, during field practices
as well as on the battlefield.**

118. The foregoing aspects of the fight,
afford an ample variety of exercises. The

principles of deployment for attack, defence, retreat, or execution of a turning movement, with or without flank protection from other troops or the ground, combined with changes of front, and transition from one tactical operation into another, finally, with or without taking the formation of the ground into account, should be represented, practised, and clearly inculcated on the drill ground, under the supposition of the simplest possible situations of war.

119. It is the duty of Commanders to practise all the principles laid down by these Regulations during the period of training at their disposal. The variation of the assumed situation furthers tactical training. Practising particular representations of the fight is prohibited.

120. The Inspecting Officer prescribes a task to be performed at the Inspection. It it only in this manner that he is enabled to form a correct opinion as to the thoroughness of the tactical training of the troops, and especially of that of officers of all grades.

121. It should be borne in mind that the formations and principles laid down only deal with the simplest cases, and, owing to change of circumstances, will frequently experience

modification when applied in the presence of the enemy. In the event of this being necessary owing to the nature of the fight, all Commanders each one in his own sphere, should be practised to adapt their plans rapidly and without hesitation to any situation, and should always realise that **omission and neglect will form a heavier indictment against them, than a mistake in the selection of adopted means.** Adherence to certain formations, should never be allowed to divert their attention from essentials.

122. The aim of all exercises, as well as of the whole course of training, should be to preserve and foster the existing predilection for the offensive.

As soon as a fair field of fire is obtained, and circumstances do not point to the necessity of bringing the fight to an immediate conclusion, the Infantry should endeavour to reap to the full the great advantage to be derived from a steady fire of troops in position. It should therefore bé accustomed, at any moment and at every turn of the fight, rapidly, if even only temporarily, to develop its fire-action to its highest possible intensity, in order to be able subsequently to attack the enemy with all the more energy and effect.

123. During the field practices of the larger units the **husbanding of the men's strength at the right time** should receive due consideration. This point should receive constant attention, all the more because the troops may when necessary, be required to fight regardless of odds,to exert themselves to the utmost, and to exhibit entire self-sacrifice.

124. The larger the scale of the fight, the greater the **scope for individual action.** The attention of Commanders should be devoted more to carrying out their special task as a whole, than to the supervision of details. The attainment of any object by the employment of uniform means on the part of the several units, should not therefore be considered of any importance. But **the scope allowed to subordinate leaders, should never be permitted to interfere with the plans of the Commander, and under all circumstances the maintenance of tactical order and the internal cohesion of the troops should be insisted upon.**

125. The more advanced practices with mixed units, and even tactical exercises in which the presence of the various arms is supposed, produce tactical situations, and call forth decisions which are far beyond the scope of these Regulations. These Regulations in no way exhaust tactical instruction ; they confine themselves to dealing with the fundamental rules. But the troops will be able, even in action, to cope with any possible task, if they have, by practice, mastered the rules contained in these Regulations.

Their training may properly be considered as successfully accomplished, **when they are capable of performing what is required in war, and when no part of what has been taught on the drill ground, has to be unlearnt on the battle-field.**

APPENDIX I.

Strength of German Units (Combatants).

Unit.	Peace Strength.				War Strength.			
	Officers.	N.C.Os.	Buglers and Drummers.	Privates.	Officers.	N.C.Os.	Buglers and Drummers.	Privates.
Company ..	4	27	4	110	5	44	4	202
Battalion ..	18	566			22	1002		
Regiment—								
3 Batts. ..	58	1709			68	3017		
4 Batts. ..	76	2263			90	4019		
Brigade ..	(Two or three Regiments.)				138	6037		

APPENDIX II.

Zug   = 2 Half Züge (subdivided into sections of not more than 6 and
not less than 4 files each).

Company = 3 Züge.
Battalion = 4 Companies.
Regiment = 3 or 4 Battalions.
Brigade   = 2 Regiments (3 in some cases).

APPENDIX III.

Normal Formations.

Züge, Companies, Battalions, Regiments, are
always numbered Right to Left.   The distances
between Züge and Companies in all Column
Formations, are invariably 7 paces.

A.—Company Formations.

In two ranks.
1. Line.
2. Company Column. No. 1 Zug in the centre.
No. 2 leading.

B.—*Battalion Formations.*

The Companies in Battalion are always in Company Column.

1. Double Column
{
1st and 3rd Companies abreast; No. 1 on the right, with 2nd and 4th in rear. This formation is adopted for purposes of assembly, and for movements outside the sphere of the enemy's fire.
}

2. Deep Column
{
Companies form up in rear of one another. No. 1 in front; remainder in succession to the rear.
Used for purposes of assembly, when a narrow front is required, or when a march is to be commenced from the point of assembly.
}

3. Broad Column
{
The Companies are formed up in line of compy. cols.
Used for parade purposes, and when the intended deployment demands a greater extent of front than of depth. It is not suited for executing Battalion changes of front. It is always adopted for re-assembling after a fight, unless otherwise ordered.
}

C.—*Regimental Formations.*

Battalions are usually formed in Double Column, in one or two lines. If composed of 3 Battalions, 2 are in front, and 1 in rear of the centre. 20 paces interval between Battalions, 30 paces distance between lines.

D.—*Brigade Formations.*

1. In wings. Regiments in mass of "Battalion Double Columns," formed up alongside each other.
2. In line. The junior Regiment in front.

Intervals and distances are the same as for the Regiment.